CONTENTS

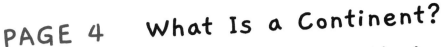

WHAT IS A CONTINENT?

A continent is a large area of land. There are seven continents on Earth. The continents are surrounded by five oceans.

North America

Arctic Ocean

Europe

Asia

Atlantic Ocean

South America

Africa

Pacific Ocean

Indian Ocean

Antarctica

Australia

Southern Ocean

4

The **population** of Earth lives on the seven continents. Each continent has different types of **landscape** and weather. There are lots of different **cultures** and people, all with different ways of living.

Let's learn about South America!

WELCOME TO SOUTH AMERICA!

Where on Earth is South America? South America is a continent that is south of North America. It is also joined to North America and is surrounded by two oceans.

Temple Kalasasaya ruins in Tiwanaku, Bolivia

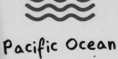
Pacific Ocean

Atlantic Ocean

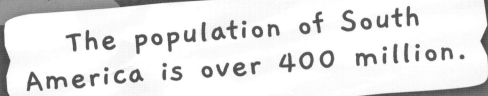

The population of South America is over 400 million.

There are 12 countries in South America. Some of the countries in South America are a part of countries that are in other continents.

Monumento Mitad in Ciudad Mitad del Mundo, Ecuador

Christ the Redeemer statue in Rio de Janeiro, Brazil

LANGUAGES IN SOUTH AMERICA

There are lots of different languages spoken in South America. Many languages were brought to South America as people from around the world moved to the continent.

Let's learn how to say 'hello' in some languages that are spoken in South America!

RIMAYKULLAYKI
QUECHUA

OLÁ
PORTUGUESE

HOLA
SPANISH

HELLO
ENGLISH

MBA'ÉICHAPA
GUARANÍ

GOEDENDAG
DUTCH

How many languages
can you speak?

SOUTH AMERICAN WEATHER

The Equator runs through the middle of the Earth. Places that are farther away from the Equator are colder than places that are closer.

Most of South America is south of the Equator.

Equator

The **climate** across South America is very different. Some parts of South America are hot and rainy and other parts can be dry and desert-like.

Amazon rainforest in Brazil

Atacama desert in Chile

There are four seasons in South America — winter, spring, summer and autumn.

Fact File:
COLOMBIA

Colombia is in the north
of South America.
There are lots of
different types of
landscapes in Colombia.

Colombia

Caribbean Sea

Pacific Ocean

Bogotá

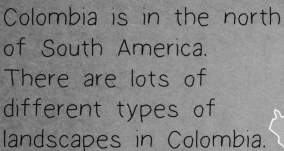

12

There are **mountain ranges** in the west of the country. There are also **cloud forests** in Colombia.

Mountains in Colombia

Cloud forest

Fact File:

Population:
Over 50 million

Biggest city:
Bogotá
(over 7 million people)

Tallest mountain:
The Pico Cristóbal Colón
(5,775 metres)

SOUTH AMERICAN ANIMALS

There are many types of animals in South America. Many of them are **adapted** to live there.

Alpacas live near mountains in Peru, Chile, Ecuador and Bolivia. They have thick fur to keep warm in winter.

Alpaca

Sloths can be found in rainforests. They are very slow animals. They have long claws that help them to hang from the treetops.

Sloth

Fact File:
BRAZIL

Brazil

Brazil is the largest
country in South America.
Many people in Brazil
live in cities and towns.

Brasilia

~~~
Atlantic
Ocean

Favelas are small towns that are in some Brazilian cities. **Indigenous** people live in villages.

Brazilian city and favela

Indigenous village

Fact File:

Population:
Over 210 million

Biggest city:
São Paulo
(over 11 million people)

Tallest mountain:
Pico da Neblina
(2,995 metres)

PLANTS and TREES

The Amazon rainforest is in eight countries, but most of it is in Brazil. It is the biggest rainforest in the world and is home to many animals and thousands of types of plant and tree.

Lobster claw flower

Chocolate comes from cocoa trees like this.

A lot of trees are being cut down in the Amazon rainforest.

Some parts of Argentina have a cold and dry climate. Cacti plants often grow in these areas.

Cacti

Fact File: CHILE

Chile is one of the longest countries in the world. Chile has lots of different landscapes. The Andes mountain range runs along the west of the country.

Chilean Sea

Santiago

Chile

Atlantic Ocean

Pacific Ocean

The dry Atacama desert is in the north of Chile. There are **glaciers** in the south of Chile where it is colder.

Atacama desert

Glaciers

Fact File:

Population:
Over 18 million

Biggest city:
Santiago
(over 6 million people)

Longest river:
Loa river
(440 kilometres)

SOUTH AMERICAN FOOD

There are many different dishes to eat in South America. Let's take a look at a few!

Empanadas are a popular meat-filled pastry enjoyed in Argentina.

Arepas are made from corn and are eaten in Colombia and Venezuela.

Dulce de leche is a dessert made from milk that is enjoyed all over South America.

Picarones are a tasty fried dessert eaten in Peru.

GLOSSARY

adapted	changed over time to suit the environment
climate	the common weather in a certain place
cloud forests	forests that get a lot of rain and have clouds in the treetops
cultures	the traditions, ideas and ways of life of groups of people
glaciers	extremely large amounts of ice that move slowly
indigenous	the first people to live in a place
landscape	how the land is laid out
mountain ranges	groups of mountains in the same area
population	the number of people living in a certain area, such as a city or country

INDEX